MY SECOND
MUSIC THEORY BOOK

Lina Ng

© RHYTHM MP SDN. BHD.1985
U.S. Edition: 2010

Published by
RHYTHM MP SDN. BHD.
1947, Lorong IKS Bukit Minyak 2, Taman IKS Bukit Minyak,
14100 Simpang Ampat, Penang, Malaysia.
Tel: +60 4 5050246 (Direct Line), +60 4 5073690 (Hunting Line)
Fax: +60 4 5050691
E-mail: rhythmmp@mphsb.com
www.rhythmmp.com

Cover Design by
Lim Wai Fun

ISBN 10: 967 98560 6 2
ISBN 13: 978 967 98560 6 4
Order No.: MPM-3002-02US

CONTENTS

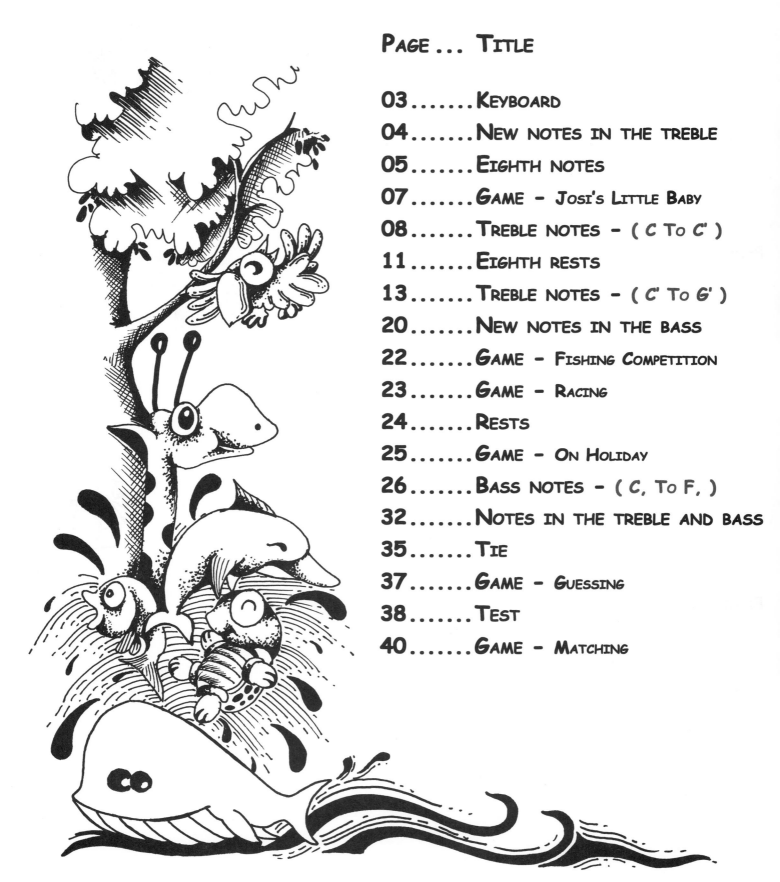

Print the letter-names on all the white keys.

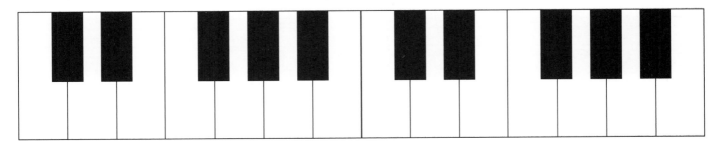

Print the letter-names.

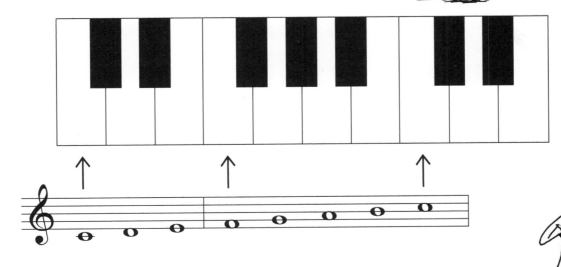

Print the letter-names and write the notes.

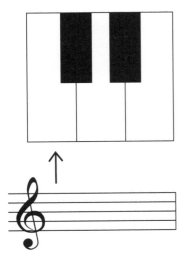

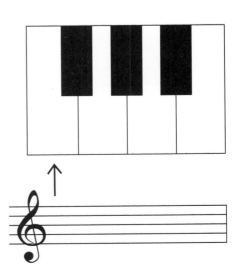

NEW NOTES IN THE TREBLE

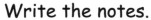

Write the notes.

C   D   E   F   G

Name the notes.

Write the notes F G A B C

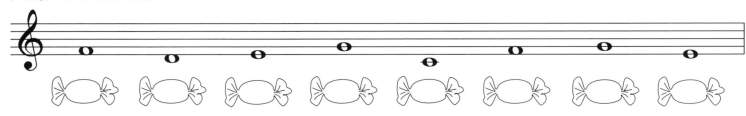

F   G   A   B   C

F   G   A   B   C

Name the notes.

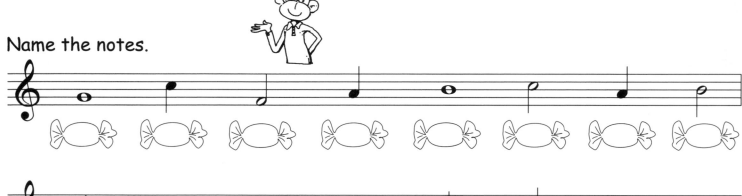

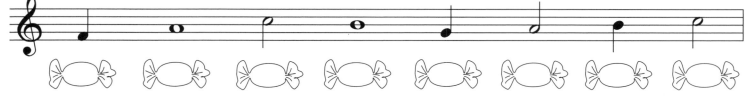

EIGHTH NOTES

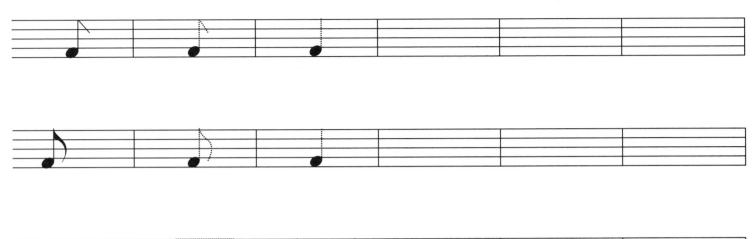

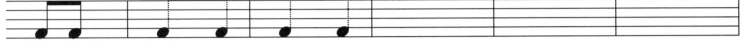

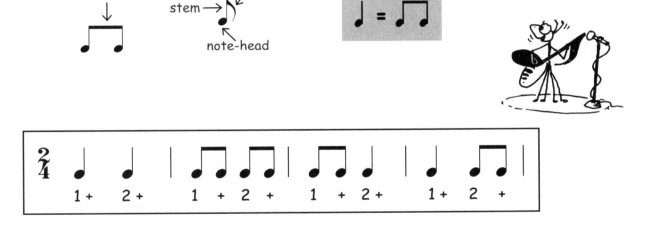

beam

stem → tail

note-head

♩ = ♫

Write the counts.

1 + 2 +

My

Complete each measure with

Write the counts.

1 + 2   3   1 2   3 +

JOSI'S LITTLE BABY

Josi's little baby is lost.

Help Josi find her baby by following the notes o ♩ ♩ ♪

Aha, Josi is a _____ (duck, cat, rabbit)

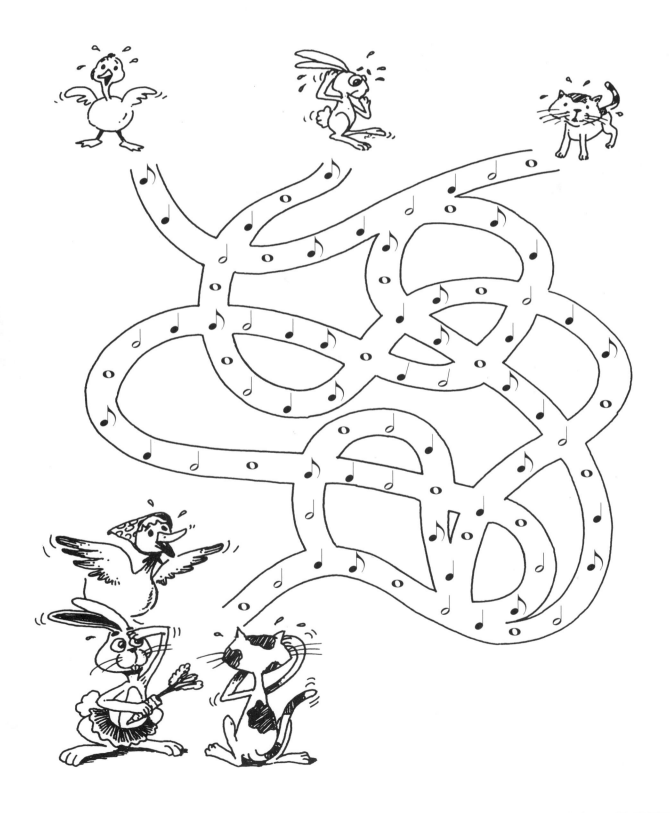

TREBLE NOTES

(C TO C')

Write the notes C - C'.

C D E F G A B C

Name the notes.

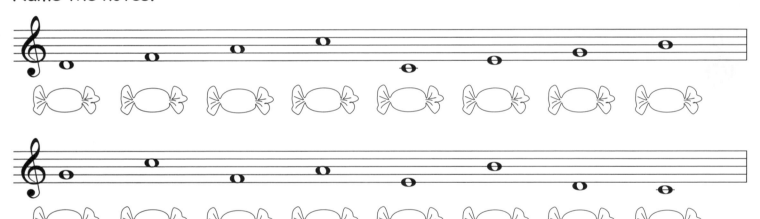

Write the notes.

G   D   C   A   B   E   F   A

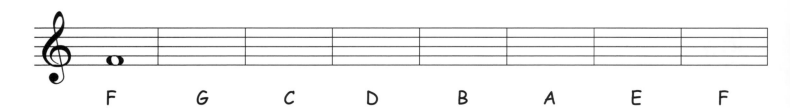

F   G   C   D   B   A   E   F

My

Write the time signatures and name the notes.

F

C

Add a stem to every note and name the notes.

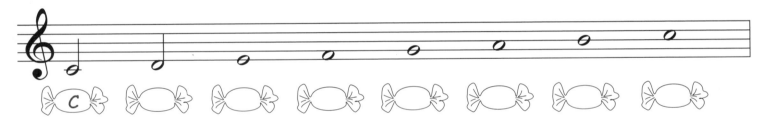

C

Add a stem to every note and write the counts.

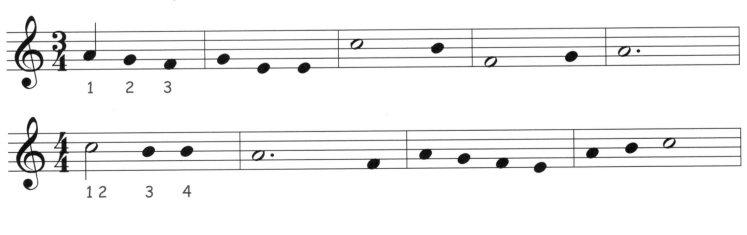

1   2   3

1 2   3   4

1   2   3 4

Match the boxes.

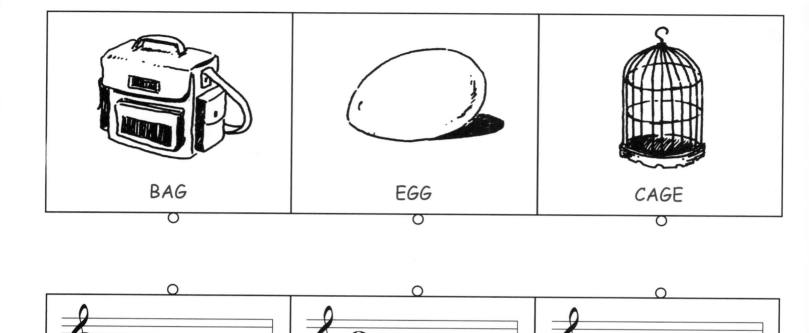

BAG

EGG

CAGE

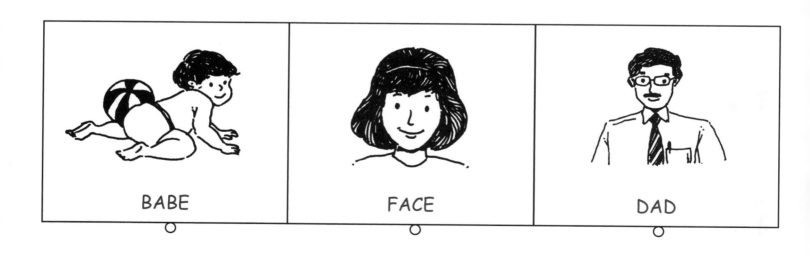

BABE

FACE

DAD

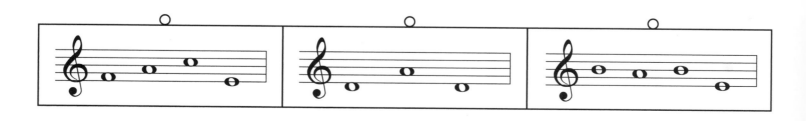

Counts: ½   ½   ½

Write the number of counts.

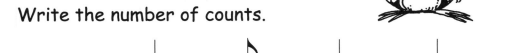

| 4 | | | | | | | |

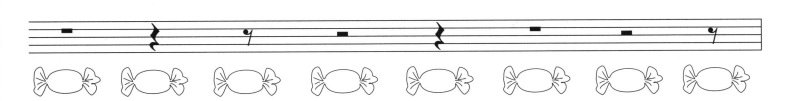

Write the counts.

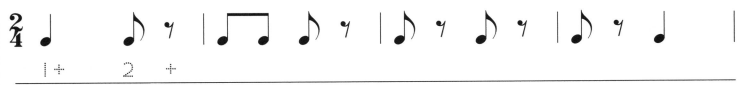

1 +   2   +

AT THE ZOO

Hello, there.
Greetings from the San Diego Zoo in California.
Each of us wears a cap.
To know the color of our caps,
look at the notes on the board.
Color accordingly.

TIME SIGNATURE	COLOR
$\frac{2}{4}$	PURPLE
$\frac{3}{4}$	GREEN
$\frac{4}{4}$	ORANGE

My

TREBLE NOTES
(C' TO G')

Write the notes `C`

Write the notes `C` `D` `E`

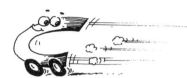

Name the notes.

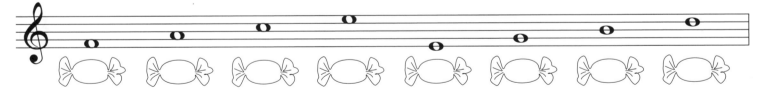

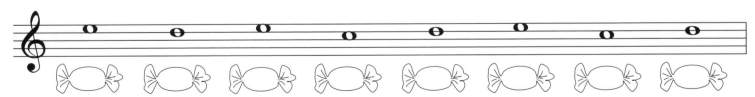

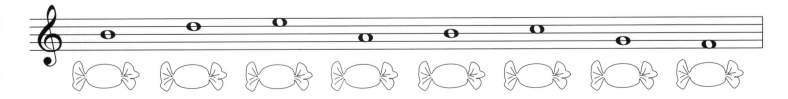

Write the notes E

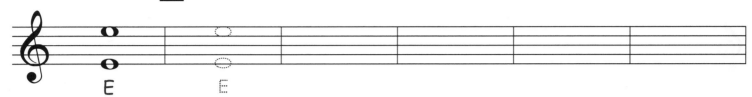

Write the notes E F G

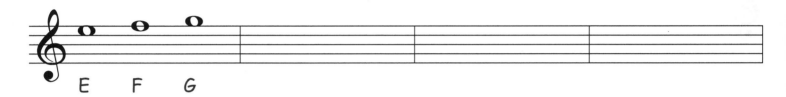

Name the notes.

Write the notes.

D   E   G   F   C   E   G   F

F   G   C   E   G   D   C   F

Add bar-lines and write the counts.

Add bar-lines and name the notes.

G

E

Match the boxes.

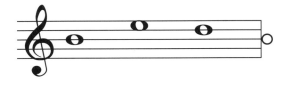

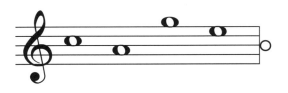

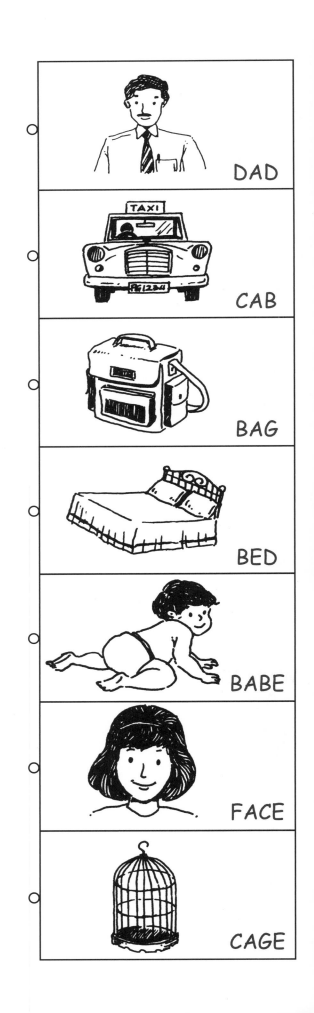

DAD

CAB

BAG

BED

BABE

FACE

CAGE

Write 1 octave (8 notes).

C D E F G A B C

D E F G A B C D

E F G A B C D E

F G A B C D E F

Write these notes 1 octave lower.

F

Write these notes 1 octave higher.

C

Complete each measure with

To which note does the accidental belong?

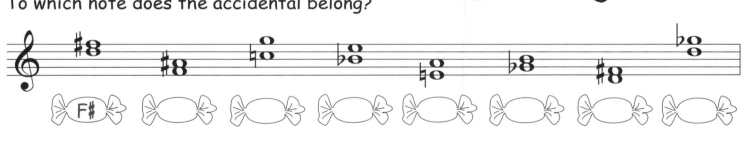

Write the printed accidental before the correct note.

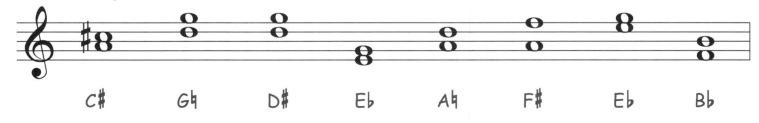

C♯   G♮   D♯   E♭   A♮   F♯   E♭   B♭

Print the letter-names on the white keys.

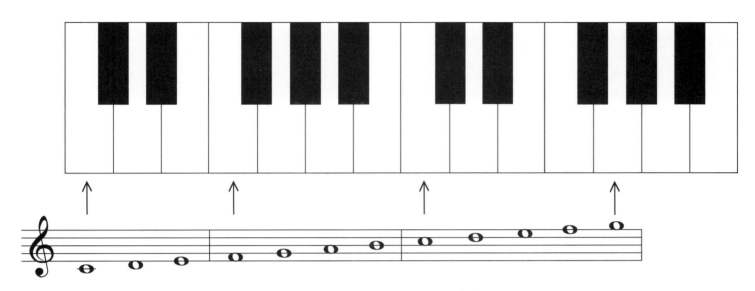

Match the notes to the keyboard.

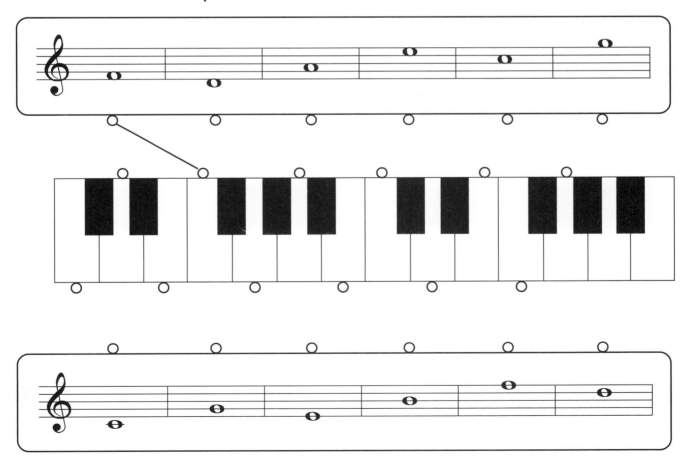

NEW NOTES IN THE BASS

Write the notes.

C   B   A   G   F

Name the notes.

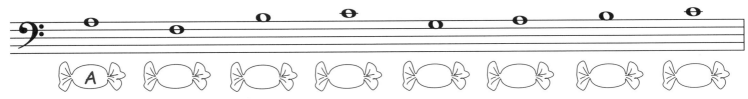

A

Write the notes   G F E D C

G   F   E   D   C

G   F   E   D   C

Name the notes.

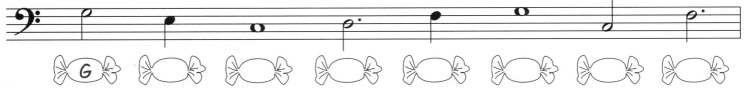

G

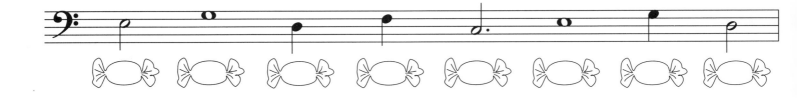

Write the notes C - C.

C   B   A   G   F   E   D   C

Name the notes.

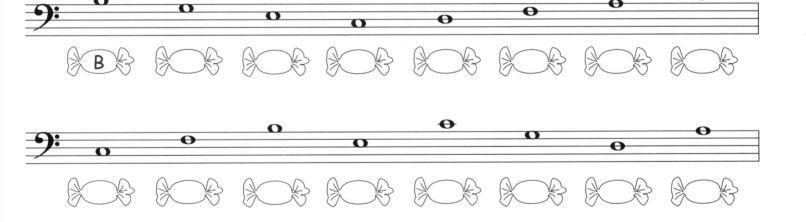

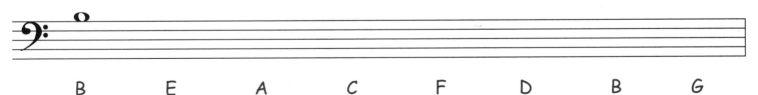

Write the notes.

B   E   A   C   F   D   B   G

F   G   C   B   D   E   A   C

FISHING COMPETITION

Wow, a fishing competition.

Who has caught:

1) an octopus - Mr._____
2) a prawn - Mr._____
3) a crab - Mr._____
4) a fish - Mr._____
5) a boot - Mr._____

RACING

Mr. BAA, Mr. FEB, Mr. DEC and Mr. BEE are having a race.
To know the results, follow the tracks. Match the results to the winners.

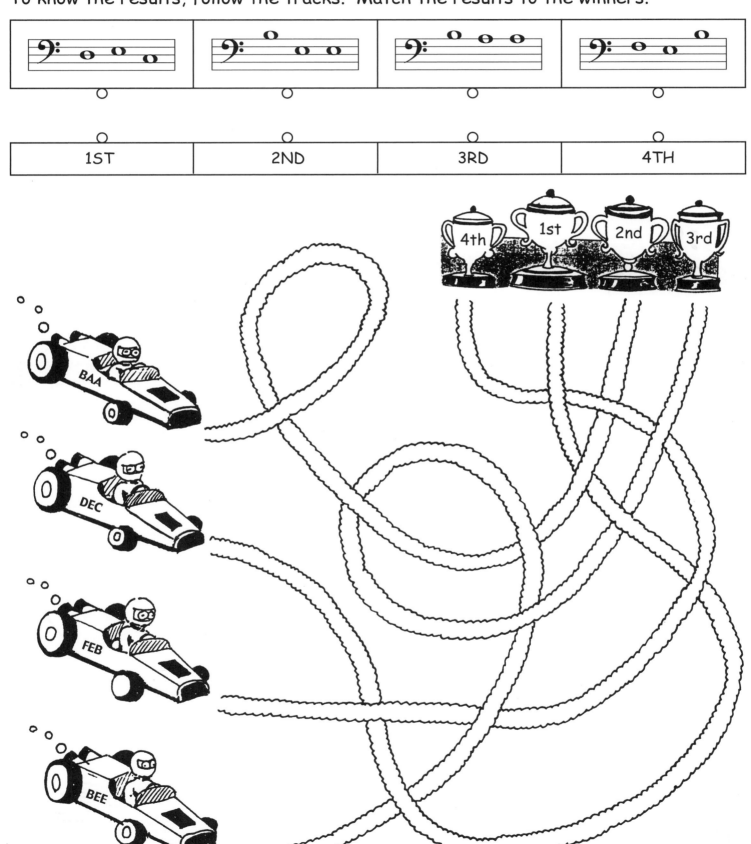

| 1ST | 2ND | 3RD | 4TH |

RESTS

Write the number of counts.

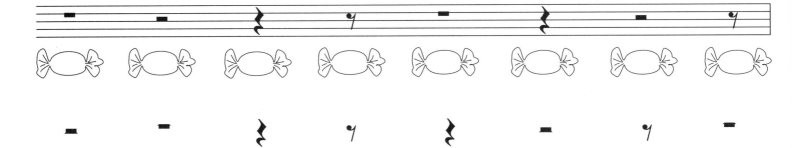

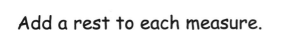

Add a rest to each measure.

ON HOLIDAY

Where do you think Mary is going for a holiday?

Follow the route | ♪ | 𝄽 | ▬ | ▬ | . Mary is going to _____ .

AMERICA

ENGLAND

AUSTRALIA

BASS NOTES
(C, to F,)

Write the notes [C]

C

Write the notes [C][B][A]

C   B   A

C   B   A

Name the notes.

C

Write the notes A G F

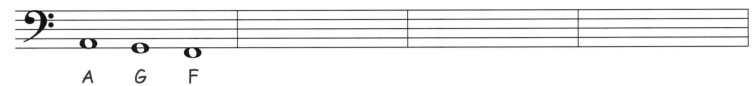

A G F

A G F

A G F

Name the notes.

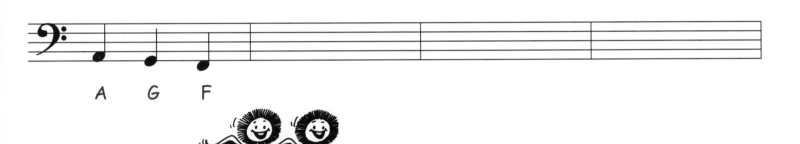

C

Write the notes.

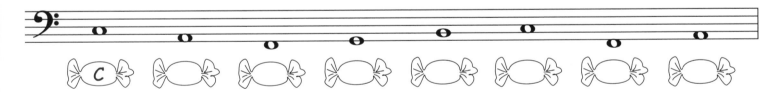

F   A   C   E   D   B   G   C

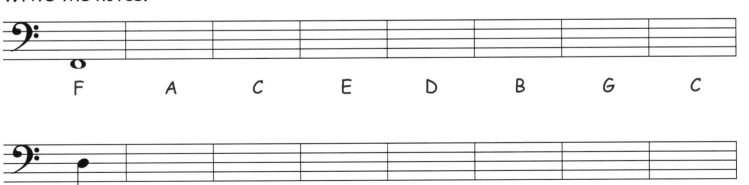

D   F   C   A   G   D   F   E

Color on the keyboard the notes you have to play.

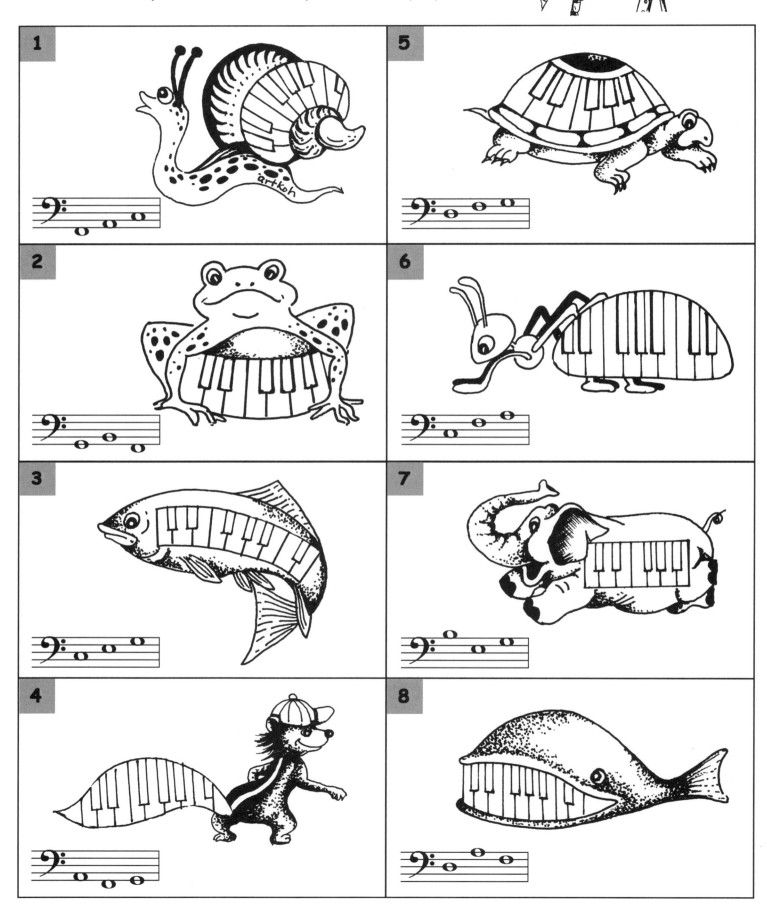

Add bar-lines and write the counts.

Add bar-lines and name the notes.

G

Match the boxes.

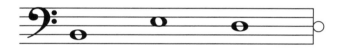

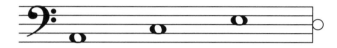

Write 1 octave (8 notes)

F G A B C D E F

G A B C D E F G

A B C D E F G A

Write these notes 1 octave lower.

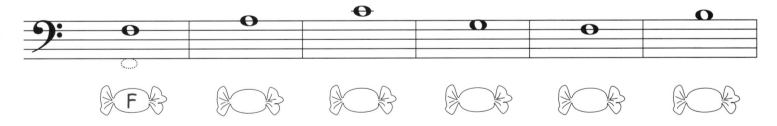

F

Write these notes 1 octave higher.

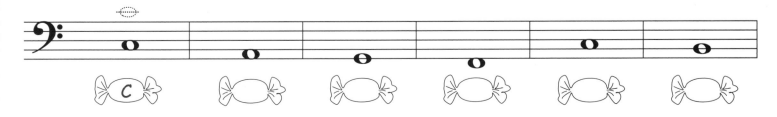

C

NOTES IN THE TREBLE AND BASS

1) Write the letter-names on the keyboard.
2) Write all the missing notes in the staff.

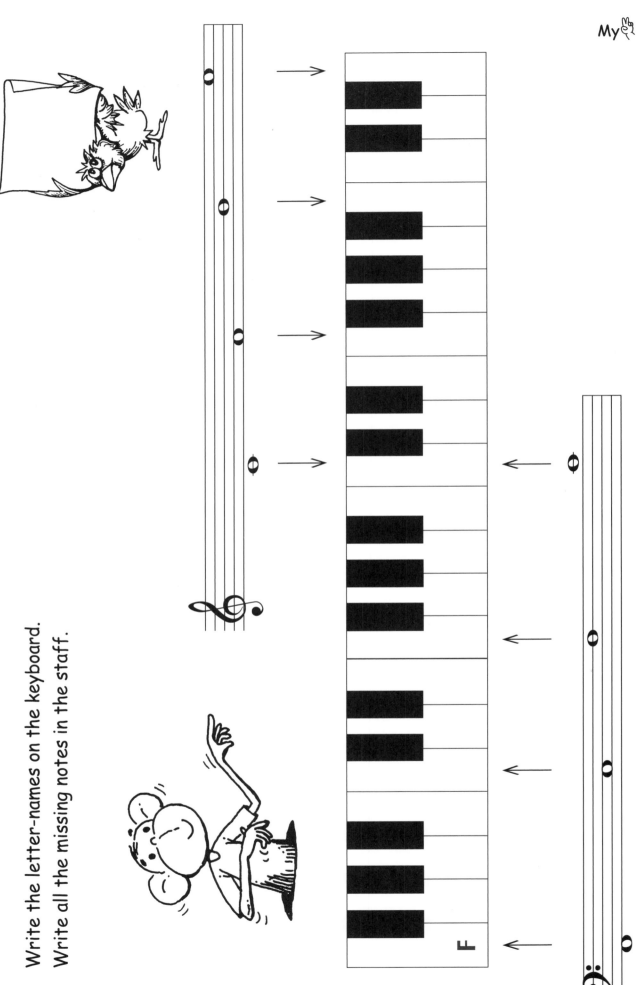

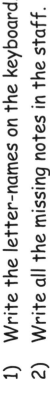

My

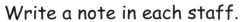

Write a note in each staff.

E D G E	F A D E	B E E F

Write the letter-names and then write the notes 1 octave lower in the bass.

C

Write the letter-names and then write the notes 1 octave higher in the treble.

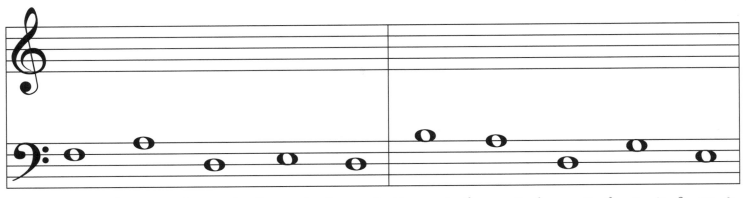

F

Match the boxes (Rest = R).

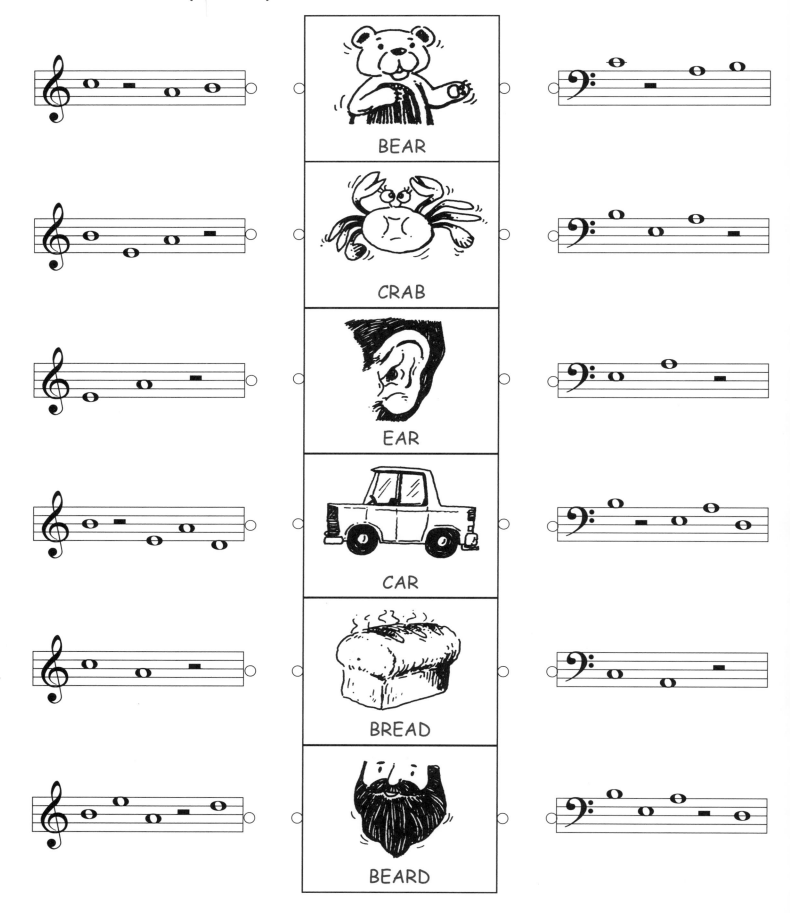

A tie joins 2 notes on the same line or space.

When 2 notes are tied,
the 2nd note is not sounded but held.

Write the counts and cross the notes that are not sounded.

Counts: 1   2   3   4

Counts:

Counts:

Counts:

Join the stems with a beam to make the correct number of beats.

Counts: 1   2

Counts:

Counts:

_____

Change some notes into quarters (♩) to make the correct number of beats.

Counts: 1   2   3

Counts:

Counts:

GUESSING

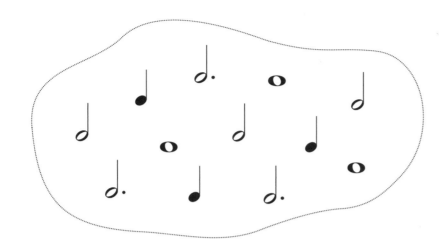

And The Winner Is

At one glance, can you guess the number of counts? Write your answer in your box.
Happy, Grumpy and Sleepy have all written their answers.

Happy's answer is the nearest. Grumpy's answer is the 2nd nearest. Poor Sleepy, he
is way out. What about you?

Can you write the names of Happy, Grumpy, Sleepy and yourself in the correct
boxes? Next, write the name of the winner in the box provided.

 **TesT**

My

TOTAL POINTS	
100	

NAME: _____

DATE: _____

1. Name the notes.

20	

2. Write a note in each staff.

20	

B   A   D   G   E   F   A   C   E   D

3. Complete each measure with 𝅗𝅥. 𝅗𝅥 𝅘𝅥

20	

*   *   *   *   *

*   *   *   *   *

4.   Add bar-lines. | 10 | |

5.   Write the notes 1 octave lower. | 10 | |

C   E   F   D   G   C

6.   Write the time signatures and counts. | 20 | |

Counts: **1**   **2**

Counts: **1**

MATCHING

(2 - 4 players)

1) Cut out the 44 cards on the back cover.

2) Turn them facedown and mix, or put them into a box.

3) Each player takes 6 cards.

4) Open 1 card to start the game. Example:
   The rest become the stack for drawing additional cards.

5) The 1st player tries to match his card to one end of the opened card.

   Example:  or

6) The 2nd player tries to match his card to either end.

7) If a player cannot match at either ends, he will have to draw a card from the stack.

8) When the row gets too long, join the 2 end cards and continue with the game.

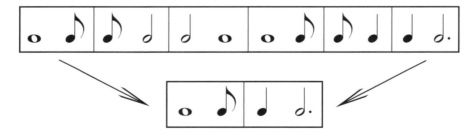

9) The player with no card left is the winner.

YiPPEEEE!